## So wird es gemacht:

Öffne das LÜK®-Kontrollgerät und lege die Plättchen in den unbedruckten Deckel. Jetzt kannst du auf den Plättchen und auf der Bodenplatte die Zahlen [1] bis [24] sehen.

**Beispiel:** Seite 2 **Irregular Plural Forms**
Nimm ein Plättchen — z.B. das Plättchen [1] und lies Aufgabe 1: one child. Wähle nun aus den beiden Antworten rechts die richtige aus! Es ist: twelve children. Daneben steht die 11. Das ist die Feldzahl, auf der du das Plättchen ablegen mußt. Lege also das Plättchen [1] auf die Zahl 11 der Bodenplatte! Die Zahl **1** muß nach oben zeigen.

| | | | | | |
|---|---|---|---|---|---|
| 1 | 2 | 3 | 4 | 5 | 6 |
| 7 | 8 | 9 | 10 | 11 | 12 |
| 13 | 14 | 15 | 16 | 17 | 18 |
| 19 | 20 | 21 | 22 | 23 | 24 |

So mußt du weiterarbeiten, bis alle Plättchen auf der Bodenplatte liegen. Schließe dann das Gerät und lege es herum. Öffne es von der Rückseite! Wenn du das bei der Übungsreihe abgebildete Muster siehst, hast du alle Aufgaben richtig gelöst. Passen einige Plättchen nicht in das Muster, dann hast du dort Fehler gemacht.

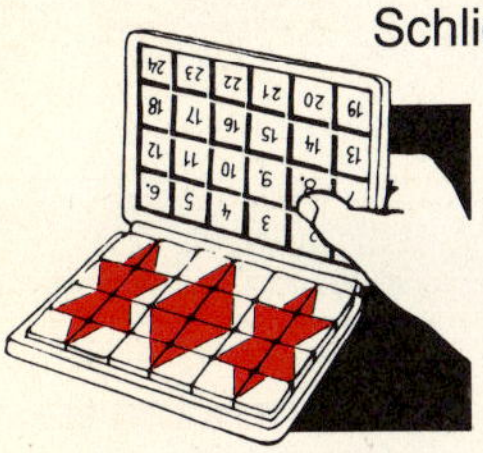

Wende diese Plättchen dort, wo sie liegen, um, schließe den Kasten, lege ihn herum und öffne ihn wieder! Nun kannst du sehen, welche Aufgaben du falsch gelöst hast. Nimm jetzt diese Plättchen heraus und suche die richtigen Ergebnisse! Kontrolliere dann noch einmal! Stimmt jetzt das Muster?

## Und nun viel Spaß!



Dieses Papier wurde aus chlorfrei gebleichtem Zellstoff hergestellt

## Irregular Plural Forms

*Was ist die richtige unregelmäßige Pluralform?*
*(Vorsicht: Manche Pluralformen haben regelmäßige Bildungen!)*

| | | | | |
|---|---|---|---|---|
| 1 | one child | | twelve child · 20 | twelve children · 11 |
| 2 | one goose | | two geese · 7 | two goose · 3 |
| 3 | one piece of cake | | two pieces of cake · 22 | two piece of cake · 14 |
| 4 | one rabbit | | five rabbits · 12 | five rabbit · 24 |
| 5 | one piece of furniture | | six pieces of furniture · 16 | six piece of furniture · 18 |
| 6 | one life | | two life · 10 | two lives · 8 |
| 7 | one mouse | | two mice · 2 | two mouse · 15 |
| 8 | one blazer | | two blazer · 1 | two blazers · 6 |
| 9 | one ticket | | eleven tickets · 21 | eleven ticket · 18 |
| 10 | one ox | | eight ox · 19 | eight oxen · 15 |
| 11 | one bike | | six bike · 13 | six bikes · 5 |
| 12 | one lamp | | seven lamp · 14 | seven lamps · 1 |
| 13 | one tooth | | ten teeth · 24 | ten tooth · 21 |
| 14 | one knife | | seven knife · 3 | seven knives · 20 |
| 15 | one clock | | two clock · 4 | two clocks · 10 |
| 16 | one scarf | | four scarf · 2 | four scarves · 23 |
| 17 | one foot | | two feet · 13 | two foot · 22 |
| 18 | one man | | nine men · 9 | nine man · 7 |
| 19 | one shelf | | two shelf · 5 | two shelves · 14 |
| 20 | one thief | | three thief · 19 | three thieves · 17 |
| 21 | one loaf of bread | | two loaf of bread · 8 | two loaves of bread · 3 |
| 22 | one wolf | | ten wolves · 19 | ten wolf · 16 |
| 23 | one woman | | two woman · 16 | two women · 18 |
| 24 | one wife | | two wife · 6 | two wives · 4 |

## Whose *(wessen)*?

*Der s-Genitiv zeigt uns, wem etwas gehört.*
*Bildung: Substantiv im Singular* = 's → the boy = the boy's book,
*Substantiv mit Plural-s* = s' → the boys = the boys' jackets,
*Substantive im Plural, die nicht auf -s enden* = 's → children = children's games.

| | | | |
|---|---|---|---|
| 1 | [Bob] car is faster than Speedy's car. | Bob's · 17 | Bobs' · 12 |
| 2 | Give me [Sally] exercise-book, please! | Sally's · 1 | Sallys' · 4 |
| 3 | The [Smiths] house is almost a palace. | Smith's · 5 | Smiths' · 10 |
| 4 | The [boys] voices are louder than a train. | boy's · 9 | boys' · 6 |
| 5 | The [porters] uniforms are not very clean. | porters'3 | porter's · 19 |
| 6 | That [porter] uniform isn't dirty at all. | porter's · 14 | porters' · 2 |
| 7 | Whose club is this? It is [Caveman]. | Caveman's · 7 | Cavemans' · 8 |
| 8 | [Doctors] coats aren't always white. | Doctors' · 23 | Doctor's · 12 |
| 9 | The [pupils] tests flew out the window. | pupil's · 11 | pupils' · 9 |
| 10 | The [dog] tail was under the chair. | dogs' · 21 | dog's · 4 |
| 11 | My [horse] tail is longer than the dog's. | horses' · 20 | horse's · 12 |
| 12 | The cat is biting the [mouse] tail. | mouse's · 20 | mouses' · 13 |
| 13 | [Patrica] birthday party was great. | Patrica's · 5 | Patricas' · 15 |
| 14 | The [parents] meeting lasted 3 hours. | parents' · 13 | parent's · 1 |
| 15 | A [fireman] job can be dangerous. | firemans' · 3 | fireman's · 21 |
| 16 | The [professors] work was important. | professor's · 6 | professors' · 18 |
| 17 | The [professor] socks had holes. | professor's · 19 | professors' · 8 |
| 18 | [Rose] brother hates pop music. | Roses' · 24 | Rose's · 22 |
| 19 | The [team] coach was fatter than Freddie. | team's · 8 | teams' · 9 |
| 20 | The [men] hats were cowboy hats. | men's · 11 | mens' · 16 |
| 21 | A [child] teddy bear is important. | childs' · 4 | child's · 15 |
| 22 | The [children] toys were upstairs. | children's · 2 | childrens' · 7 |
| 23 | That [girl] bikini is pink and yellow. | girls' · 12 | girl's · 24 |
| 24 | Whose cola is this? It is [Tom] cola. | Tom's · 16 | Toms' · 14 |

## Looking for Adjectives: The Pink Cassette

*Ein Adjektiv bezieht sich auf ein Substantiv und hat im Gegensatz zum Deutschen keine Endungen.*

(adj.) (noun)
This is an easy sentence.

***Finde die Adjektive!***

1 It was a [sunny · 4] [afternoon · 18].

2 Marty and his [fat · 19] friend were at the [playground · 2].

3 They brought [their · 21] [new · 24] table-tennis bats with them.

4 A [crowd · 16] of [young · 3] children was there too.

5 They were [running · 12] around in [big · 11] circles.

6 It was a [wonderful · 20] game and lots of [fun · 1].

7 Then [they · 6] all heard a [loud · 7] noise.

8 Two boys in [black · 15] [jackets · 21] rode in on a motorcycle.

9 [They · 14] were listening to [“heavy metal” · 23] music.

10 The [motorcycle · 22] had [comfortable · 12] leather seats.

11 The [mysterious · 16] boys stopped in front of the [children · 5].

12 They wanted to play a quick · 8 game · 17 of ping-pong.

13 They didn't have nice · 9 bats · 23.

14 Marty's frightened · 13 friend hid behind · 19 a girl.

15 The fair-haired · 17 girl laughed · 5 at him.

16 "Don't be a · 18 silly · 10 boy", she said.

17 "Nobody · 7 is going to take your super · 1 bat.

18 Listen, I · 16 have a wonderful · 18 idea!

19 I want to listen to my · 6 new · 2 cassette.

20 They can borrow · 8 your fine · 22 bats.

21 We can · 3 use their expensive · 5 cassette-player."

22 Now the girl is telling · 20 the boys her lovely · 14 idea.

23 She · 7 takes out a pink · 21 disco cassette.

24 They see · 4 the terrible · 6 cassette and drive off.

## Comparing Things at the Fleamarket

*Ein Adjektiv kann seine Grundform (Positiv) ändern, wenn man einen Vergleich anstellt. Diese Vergleichsform (Komparativ) bildet oder steigert man mit -er:*
Tuesday was warm, but Wednesday was warmer.

*Bei* ***Gleichheit*** *gibt es jedoch keine Steigerung:*
Martin is as old as Kevin. *(... so alt wie ...)*

*Bei* ***Ungleichheit*** *verwendet man den Komparativ mit* "than":
Caveman is older than Kevin. *(... älter als ...)*

| | | | |
|---|---|---|---|
| 1 | The fleamarket is | cheaper than · 16 / as cheaper as · 9 | a department store. |
| 2 | Winter coats are | warmer as · 21 / warmer than · 24 | summer coats. |
| 3 | Those shoes are | as dirty as · 19 / dirty than · 13 | these shoes here. |
| 4 | That woman over there is | happier than · 15 / happier as · 2 | this person here. |
| 5 | She is | thinner than · 7 / thinner as · 22 | fat Freddy. |
| 6 | The parrot's cage was | as dirtier as · 20 / dirtier than · 23 | the rabbit's cage. |
| 7 | That man's ladder is | longer than · 11 / longer as · 12 | Mr. Wang's ladder. |
| 8 | He can hang his goods | higher as · 14 / higher than · 3 | Mr. Wang. |
| 9 | The puppet show is | as funny as · 20 / funnier as · 14 | the clown. |
| 10 | They are both | as funnier as · 1 / funnier than · 8 | a TV show. |

| | | | |
|---|---|---|---|
| 11 | I'm | as hungry as · 4<br>as hungrier as · 9 | a horse. |
| 12 | Those hot dogs look | nicer as · 18<br>nicer than · 12 | the sausages. |
| 13 | This tomato soup is | hotter as · 5<br>hotter than · 21 | the Irish stew. |
| 14 | Less salt in your food is | as healthier as · 20<br>healthier than · 17 | more salt. |
| 15 | Hamburgers with ketchup are | tastier as · 1<br>tastier than · 13 | beans. |
| 16 | Cold chocolate milk is | as good as · 22<br>better as · 6 | a milk shake. |
| 17 | A milk shake is | better as · 17<br>better than · 6 | cold coffee. |
| 18 | This picture here is | as prettier as · 15<br>prettier than · 14 | that one over there. |
| 19 | Those stamps look just | as older as · 9<br>as old as · 5 | these stamps. |
| 20 | The old records are | cheaper as · 8<br>cheaper than · 10 | the new records. |
| 21 | Second-hand clothes are not | as expensive as · 2<br>expensiver as · 16 | new clothes. |
| 22 | Those dirty socks smell | stronger as · 5<br>stronger than · 18 | a lion's cage. |
| 23 | These old comics are | funnier than · 9<br>as funnier as · 19 | the new ones. |
| 24 | But the new ones are | cleaner as · 5<br>cleaner than · 1 | the old comics. |

## "More" + Adjective

*Die Steigerung des Adjektivs kann mit* "more" *gebildet werden, wenn die Adjektive drei Silben haben:* more important.
*Bei zwei Silben kann man mit* -er (happier) *und auch* "more" *steigern.*
*Meistens wird bei Adjektiven auf* -id *und* -ct *der Komparativ mit* "more" *bevorzugt:* more correct.
*Bilde den Komparativ! Beachte die Steigerung mit* -er *oder* more*!*
**Achtung:** *Manche Adjektive lassen sich nicht steigern!*

| | | | |
|---|---|---|---|
| 1 | Bill says Sally is | more attractive · 15<br>attractiver · 18 | than Ramona. |
| 2 | Ramona thinks Mark is | as handsome as · 13<br>handsomer than · 2 | Bill. |
| 3 | Mark told me Ramona is | more beautiful · 18<br>beautiful · 19 | than Sally. |
| 4 | Sally is | more intelligent as · 1<br>as intelligent as · 16 | Ramona. |
| 5 | Ramona said Wally was not | as stupid as · 5<br>more stupid as · 21 | Blockhead. |
| 6 | Blockhead was | more stupid · 14<br>stupider · 24 | than Wally. |
| 7 | Milly's test was | difficulter · 8<br>more difficult · 1 | than Bessie's. |
| 8 | Bessie is intelligent, but Milly is | more intelligent · 3<br>intelligenter · 20 | . |
| 9 | Bessie's room is | tidier · 17<br>more tidy · 9 | than her brother's. |
| 10 | Fat Freddy is | more heavy · 22<br>heavier · 6 | than thin Timmy. |

11 This exercise is simple, but the next one is [simpler · 4 / more simple · 10] .

12 English is [more easy · 8 / easier · 2] than Russian.

13 This street is [more narrow · 23 / narrower · 21] than the other street.

14 Our class is [quieter · 19 / more quiet · 14] than the other class.

15 Our English teacher is [popularer · 11 / more popular · 23] than our Maths teacher.

16 His lessons are [more interesting · 22 / interestinger · 18] than Maths lessons.

17 The boy next to me is awful, but the boy behind me is [awful · 15 / more awful · 7] .

18 Music videos are exciting, but live music is [excitinger · 20 / more exciting · 24] .

19 Sometimes I'm nervous, but during a test I'm [nervouser · 16 / more nervous · 8] .

20 Berlin is a famous city, but London is [more famous · 9 / famouser · 17] .

21 Mother thinks wild flowers are lovely, but roses are [lovelier · 11 / more lovely · 3] .

22 Things are [wonderful · 6 / more wonderful · 20] this year.

23 This meal tastes [deliciouser · 8 / more delicious · 10] than the last meal.

24 I broke a glass and mum was [furiouser · 15 / more furious · 12] than dad.

## The Superlative (-est / most): The Thickest Fog

*Das Adjektiv wird mit Grundform* + -est *gesteigert:* → The <u>slowest</u> car in the race lost.
*Zweisilbige Adjektive, die auf* -le, -er, -ow, -y *enden, werden auch mit* -est *gesteigert:* → It was the <u>prettiest</u> watch.
*Zweisilbige Adjektive, die nicht auf* -y *enden, werden meist mit* "most" *gesteigert:* → the <u>most famous</u> building.
*Dreisilbige Adjektive steigert man mit* "most": → It was the <u>most expensive</u> watch.

***Finde den richtigen Superlativ! Achte auf die Rechtschreibung!***

| | | | |
|---|---|---|---|
| 1 | Harry owns the | biggest · 11 / most big · 3 | boat in our school. |
| 2 | He's the | more popular · 10 / most popular · 7 | boy in our class. |
| 3 | He goes sailing on the | most large · 5 / largest · 4 | boat in our district. |
| 4 | The water is the | warmer · 8 / warmest · 12 | in late summer. |
| 5 | Harry told us the | silliest · 10 / most silliest · 14 | story the other day. |
| 6 | His sister has the | most terrible · 8 / more terrible · 1 | scream of anyone. |
| 7 | Some people say her scream is the | awful · 6 / most awful · 1 | thing to hear. |
| 8 | She went sailing on the | coldest · 5 / most cold · 17 | autumn day. |
| 9 | The fog was the | thickest · 3 / most thick · 9 | anyone had ever seen. |
| 10 | Winning a game is the | more special · 2 / most special · 9 | thing for her. |

| | | | | |
|---|---|---|---|---|
| 11 | Harry and his sister were playing the | more exciting · 22 | most exciting · 6 | card game. |
| 12 | Then his sister got the | unluckiest · 2 | most unluckiest · 24 | cards and lost. |
| 13 | She cried the | most sad · 15 | saddest · 23 | tears one can cry. |
| 14 | Then she noticed a card with the | smallest · 19 | most small · 22 | mark on it. |
| 15 | Harry had played the | most dirty · 21 | dirtiest · 16 | card trick on her. |
| 16 | Harry's sister got the | most red · 14 | reddest · 24 | face ever. |
| 17 | She was certainly the | most angry · 20 | angriest · 13 | sister there could be. |
| 18 | She let out the | loudest · 15 | most loud · 19 | scream he'd ever heard. |
| 19 | Then they heard the | more urgent · 17 | most urgent · 14 | honking sound. |
| 20 | Another ship was coming at the | fastest · 17 | most fast · 18 | speed. |
| 21 | Then it made the | quickest · 21 | most quick · 20 | left turn. |
| 22 | The girl's scream was the | wonderful · 18 | most wonderful · 20 | warning. |
| 23 | It saved them from the | more awful · 22 | most awful · 18 | accident. |
| 24 | The captain said it was the | most lovely · 10 | loveliest · 22 | scream he'd heard. |

## *Positiv — Komparativ — Superlativ:*
## It's Nice Having a Twin Sister

*Tip: Gib acht auf die unregelmäßige Steigerung good — better — best! Bilde einen sinnvollen Satz mit der richtigen Steigerungsform des Adjektivs!*

1 Mrs. Holly had two | lovelier · 6 / lovely · 23 | daughters.

2 They were | nice · 19 / nicer as · 17 | twin sisters.

3 Wendy was | as pretty as · 9 / prettiest · 20 | Betty.

4 Betty was | as tall as · 24 / taller as · 15 | Wendy.

5 But Betty's hair was | dark · 7 / darker · 4 | than Wendy's.

6 Betty was also a | better · 20 / good · 11 | dancer than Wendy.

7 She was the | better · 2 / best · 13 | dancer at her school.

8 On Saturday she wanted to be in a | more famous · 14 / famous · 17 | dance contest.

9 On Saturdays she worked in an | expensive · 10 / expensivest · 22 | restaurant.

10 The restaurant manager was a | terrible · 3 / worst · 6 | person.

11 He was | worse · 21 / as bad as · 18 | a gangster.

| | | | |
|---|---|---|---|
| 12 | Wendy was | worried · 14<br>worry · 8 | that Betty could lose her job. |
| 13 | She got a | wonderful · 11<br>more wonderful · 17 | idea. |
| 14 | She could colour her hair | darker · 12<br>as dark as · 7 | Betty. |
| 15 | Betty thought it was a | better · 13<br>good · 22 | idea. |
| 16 | A waitress has to be | friendliest · 3<br>friendlier · 12 | than the customers. |
| 17 | She must be | quicker · 1<br>quickest · 23 | than a rabbit. |
| 18 | Betty didn't feel | as miserable as · 21<br>more miserable · 9 | she did before. |
| 19 | It was perhaps the | good · 20<br>best · 2 | thing they could do. |
| 20 | Not going to the dance contest was | bad · 1<br>worse · 5 | than losing her job. |
| 21 | Dancing was the | more important · 4<br>most important · 16 | thing in her life. |
| 22 | Mrs. Holly was | worried · 10<br>more worried · 8 | than the twin sisters. |
| 23 | But saying no was | most difficult · 18<br>more difficult · 6 | than saying yes. |
| 24 | So she wished them luck and hoped for the | good · 24<br>best · 15 | . |

## This, That / These, Those (The Demonstrative Adjectives)

*Tip: In Zweifelsfällen benutze diese Tabelle!*

| | Singular | Plural |
|---|---|---|
| *Wenn etwas in greifbarer Nähe ist →* | this pen | these pens (here) |
| *Wenn etwas weiter entfernt ist →* | that pen | those pens (over there) |

1 How long have you had [that · 3 | these · 19] old jacket?

2 I've only had [those · 20 | this · 5] jacket for three years.

3 [Those · 2 | These · 21] people over there are making too much noise.

4 Well, go over to [this · 24 | that · 4] policeman and tell him about it.

5 Do you see [this · 18 | that · 7] girl in the red dress?

6 Yes, she's talking to [these · 14 | those · 6] boys over there.

7 Where did you buy [those · 14 | that · 11] pair of shorts?

8 Oh Mark, [these · 15 | this · 23] flowers are so pretty.

9 This is my desk and [this · 13 | that · 1] is your desk.

10 [That · 8 | This · 10] clerk there drinks twelve cups of coffee a day.

11 Look! [These · 17 | Those · 16] children are running down the street.

12 Don't you think [these · 19 | that · 12] bed and breakfast place is nice?

13 Take [that · 7 | this · 9] book here and put it on my desk.

14 When you have finished [this · 17 | these · 1] exercise, you can play outside.

15 Give me some of [those · 13 | that · 6] tomatoes, please!

16 You can have this one and I'll take [that · 10 | these · 3] one.

17 [This · 12 | These · 23] questions are silly, aren't they?

18 It has been very cold [that · 15 | this · 14] month, hasn't it?

19 Susan, take off [this · 5 | that · 24] silly hat at once.

20 [Those · 21 | These · 8] wolves over there look like sheep.

21 The doctor told you to take two of [these · 19 | this · 11] tablets a day.

22 Don't be afraid of [that · 2 | those · 18] white mice.

23 [That · 22 | This · 4] castle over there is very old.

24 Boris played tennis with [that · 20 | these · 16] ball.

## Some and Any

<u>Some</u> *steht meistens in bejahten Sätzen.*
<u>Any</u> *steht meistens in Fragen und verneinten Sätzen.*
*In Fragesätzen bleiben* <u>some</u> *—* <u>any</u> *oft unübersetzt.*

1 Diana, do you have [some · 17 | any · 20] Irish folk records?
2 No, but I've got [some · 24 | any · 13] great disco records.
3 Let's have [some · 21 | any · 19] hamburgers for lunch.
4 Fine, but I don't want [any · 19 | some · 23] onions on them.
5 We've also got some beans and [any · 18 | some · 16] chips.
6 Mum, have we got [any · 23 | some · 15] tomatoes?
7 I'm sorry, we don't have [some · 14 | any · 18].
8 But we've got [any · 10 | some · 14] nice green salad.
9 Mum, I need [any · 12 | some · 22] new clothes.
10 I really need [any · 8 | some · 15] socks and a pair of shoes.
11 Your brother has got [some · 13 | any · 17] nice shoes for you.
12 I don't want [any · 17 | some · 11] shoes that my brother has worn!
13 Your sister can make [any · 12 | some · 8] socks for you.
14 My sister can buy [some · 12 | any · 2] socks, but she can't make them.
15 [Any · 11 | Some · 10] brothers just don't say nice things to sisters.
16 Dad doesn't have [any · 7 | some · 4] money because Sue spends it all.
17 Try to say [any · 10 | some · 6] nice things about your sister.
18 I don't know [some · 3 | any · 9].
19 Sue, your brother needs [any · 1 | some · 5] presents.
20 I want to give him [any · 4 | some · 2] new socks, mum.
21 He says he wants [any · 10 | some · 4] new shoes.
22 Doesn't he want [any · 11 | some · 21] cowboy things?
23 No, I don't have [some · 9 | any · 1] more ideas.
24 He doesn't have [some · 8 | any · 3] food for his goldfish, does he?

## What about Ice-Cream?
## (Some — Any and their Compounds)

*Die Zusammensetzungen mit* "some" *stehen meistens in bejahten Sätzen. Die Zusammensetzungen mit* "any" *stehen meistens in Fragen und Verneinungen.*
Anyone / anybody *((irgend) jemand),* anywhere *(irgendwo, bei Verneinung nirgendwo),* anything *(etwas),* someone / somebody *(jemand),* somewhere *(irgendwo (hin)),* something *(etwas).*

1 Two teenage boys can't find a job ______.

anywhere · 7 | somewhere · 2

2 They haven't found ______ who will help them.

anyone · 23 | someone · 10

3 There must be ______ who can help them.

anyone · 8 | someone · 22

4 Perhaps they can sell ______.

something · 20 | anything · 9

5 Jerry, I think we can sell ______.

anywhere · 21 | something · 16

6 Ben, we don't have ______ to sell.

something · 3 | anything · 12

7 Well my friend, do you have ______ good ideas?

any · 17 | anywhere · 18

8 Yes, we must get a job ______.

anywhere · 4 | somewhere · 1

9 Oh, give your silly ideas to ______ else!

anybody · 5 | somebody · 21

10 Stop that! Let's go ______ and have an ice-cream.

anywhere · 13 | somewhere · 15

11 Yes, but you must pay because I don't have ______ money.

some · 24 | any · 14

12 Wait, I have an idea! We can make ______ ice-cream and sell it.

| some · 6 | any · 2 |
|---|---|

13 Yes, ice-cream is ______ that everybody loves.

| something · 19 | anything · 16 |
|---|---|

14 We will need ______ milk, ice and different fruits.

| any · 7 | some · 11 |
|---|---|

15 Is there ______ else that would taste good in our ice-cream?

| any · 17 | anything · 10 |
|---|---|

16 I don't want ______ fish and chips in my ice-cream.

| any · 8 | some · 20 |
|---|---|

17 You're right. Let's put ______ in like apples and peaches.

| anything · 7 | something · 5 |
|---|---|

18 Yes, and there must be an old van ______.

| anywhere · 12 | somewhere · 9 |
|---|---|

19 I know ______ who has an old van and we can use it.

| someone · 18 | anyone · 23 |
|---|---|

20 Do you know ______ who has a white uniform?

| anyone · 13 | anywhere · 15 |
|---|---|

21 Yes, my doctor. Let's wear ______ white jeans and T-shirts.

| any · 16 | some · 3 |
|---|---|

22 Nobody will say ______ if we wear colourful clothes.

| anybody · 20 | anything · 24 |
|---|---|

23 We need ______ who'll help us find a name for our ice-cream.

| someone · 2 | anyone · 22 |
|---|---|

24 Don't worry! I've got ______ great ideas.

| some · 4 | any · 1 |
|---|---|

## A Mother and her Daughter (Auxiliary Verbs)

*Wortbedeutungen:* Can *(können),* may *(dürfen → bittet um oder erteilt Erlaubnis),* must/have to *(müssen),* must not *(nicht dürfen → verbietet etwas). Beachte:* "Must" *und* "needn't" *kann man nur im* "present tense" *verwenden! Bei anderen Zeitformen verwendet man* "to have to".

**Complete the conversation with the best auxiliary form!**

1 Mum, there's a picnic today. ( ) go, please?

Must I · 20 | Do I have to · 3 | May I · 14

2 Yes, darling you ( ) go.

must · 4 | may · 16 | needn't · 2

3 ( ) clean my room before I go?

Do I have to · 17 | Can I · 15 | Did I have to · 21

4 No, you ( ).

didn't have to · 1 | don't have to · 13 | must · 8

5 But you ( ) go with those awful friends of yours!

have to · 18 | mustn't · 5 | may · 24

6 That's terrible mum. Why ( ) go with them?

can't I · 15 | may I · 2 | do I have to · 7

7 You ( ) go with them because they drive dangerously.

needn't · 11 | can · 10 | mustn't · 3

8 Perhaps your father ( ) take you there instead.

didn't have to · 22 | mustn't · 21 | can · 1

9 Dad ( ) take me. I want to go with my friends!

needn't · 18 | must · 12 | had to · 19

10 You ( ) shout at me like that, Susan.

may · 11 | don't have to · 6 | must · 10

11 I'm sorry. ( ) I go with them if we don't drink beer?

Mustn't · 8 | Needn't · 4 | Can · 2

12 Susan, ◯ ◯ say everything twice!

| must I · 4 | can I · 11 | did I have to · 20 |
|---|---|---|

13 I'm sorry again mum, no you ◯ ◯.

| must · 24 | don't have to · 19 | can't · 7 |
|---|---|---|

14 Mum, do you know that Sally ◯ ◯ do what she wants to do?

| can · 21 | must · 15 | needn't · 22 |
|---|---|---|

15 Susan, you ◯ ◯ compare yourself to Sally.

| must · 24 | mustn't · 23 | have to · 13 |
|---|---|---|

16 When I was your age, I ◯ ◯ listen to my parents.

| must · 18 | can · 14 | had to · 20 |
|---|---|---|

17 ◯ ◯ you really talk like that mum?

| May · 15 | Must · 10 | Can · 22 |
|---|---|---|

18 Susan, I've just decided that you ◯ ◯ clean your room.

| must · 24 | may · 15 | can · 1 |
|---|---|---|

19 Please mum, ◯ ◯ be nice?

| must you · 17 | did you have to · 5 | can't you · 9 |
|---|---|---|

20 All right Susan, you ◯ ◯ go if you take a taxi.

| may · 8 | needn't · 2 | must · 11 |
|---|---|---|

21 And ◯ ◯ come along with me?

| can dad · 18 | does dad have to · 12 | may dad · 4 |
|---|---|---|

22 No, dad ◯ ◯ go, if you don't want him to.

| doesn't have to · 22 | must · 6 | can · 9 |
|---|---|---|

23 And ◯ ◯ bring my friends along in the taxi?

| mustn't I · 3 | do I have to · 14 | may I · 7 |
|---|---|---|

24 You win dear. Yes, you ◯ ◯.

| must · 16 | needn't · 9 | may · 11 |
|---|---|---|

## Adverbs of Manner

*Im Gegensatz zum Deutschen hat das Adverb meistens eine andere Form als das Adjektiv. Ein Adverb bezieht sich auf das Verb und wird mit dem Adjektiv* + -ly *gebildet.*

*(adj.)* *(adv.)*
The slow bus drove slowly.
(Man fragt danach, wie er fährt/wie etwas geschieht.)

**Put in the correct form of the adjective or adverb!**

| | | | |
|---|---|---|---|
| 1 | Wally walked to work | quickly · 19<br>quick · 24 | because he was late. |
| 2 | Linda had a | loud · 11<br>loudly · 12 | voice. |
| 3 | She laughed | loudly · 21<br>loud · 3 | at parties. |
| 4 | Mum became | angry · 8<br>angrily · 10 | when she did this. |
| 5 | She looked at her | angrily · 16<br>angry · 1 | . |
| 6 | The poor man's pockets were | empty · 24<br>emptily · 15 | . |
| 7 | The children | careful · 18<br>carefully · 5 | opened the presents. |
| 8 | Miss Doyle | nervously · 7<br>nervous · 12 | opened the telegram. |
| 9 | She was the | happy · 22<br>happily · 23 | winner of a contest. |
| 10 | The policeman answered their questions | politely · 15<br>polite · 20 | . |
| 11 | Karen solved the mystery | easy · 14<br>easily · 2 | . |

12 Remembering facts is [easy · 12 / easily · 6].

13 The mouse looked at the cat [curious · 4 / curiously · 13].

14 Then it ran into its hole [quickly · 23 / quick · 15].

15 The [hungry · 10 / hungrily · 22] cat jumped forward.

16 The boy climbed down the [dangerous · 20 / dangerously · 8] cliff.

17 Max always does things very [good · 5 / well · 17].

18 The [funny · 9 / funnily · 19] film made them laugh.

19 Matthew had a [badly · 7 / bad · 6] cold.

20 She sang the song [beautifully · 1 / beautiful · 16].

21 September usually has [good · 4 / well · 9] weather.

22 The teacher spoke to the children [quiet · 2 / quietly · 18].

23 The Indians waved their arms [wild · 11 / wildly · 14] in the air.

24 Mr. Smart answered the questions [correct · 21 / correctly · 3].

## Adverbs of Place *(Ort)* / Time *(Zeit)* / Frequency *(Häufigkeit)* / Degree *(Grad)*

*Nicht alle Adverbien sind von Adjektiven abgeleitet. Die Stellung der Adverbien ist unterschiedlich, aber meistens steht das Adverb vor dem Subjekt, vor dem Hauptverb oder am Satzende. Vorsicht, im Gegensatz zum Deutschen steht ein Adverb nie zwischen Prädikat und Objekt!*

| *Subjekt* | *Adverb* | *Prädikat* | *Objekt* | |
|---|---|---|---|---|
| Tom | often | plays | the guitar | . |

*Tom spielt oft die Gitarre.*

**Put the adverbs in the correct place!**

**1** (4) bought (3) Carol (2) sometimes (1) chocolate
15 > 3 4 2 1 — 5 > 3 2 4 1

**2** (1) has (3) Mr. Waddle (4) hardly (2) a thing (5) done
1 > 3 1 4 5 2 — 9 > 3 1 5 4 2

**3** (2) Sally's (4) just (3) has (1) train (5) left
18 > 2 1 3 5 4 — 4 > 2 1 3 4 5

**4** (3) weekly (1) eats (2) Martin (4) a beef steak
3 > 3 1 2 4 — 6 > 2 1 4 3

**5** (3) at the thermometer (1) the old lady (2) looks (4) every day
2 > 3 1 2 4 — 10 > 1 2 3 4

**6** (4) fell off (2) the cliff (1) almost (3) the mountain climber
2 > 3 1 4 2 — 7 > 3 4 1 2

**7** (4) can't (1) Mr. Spectacle (2) his glasses (3) anywhere (5) find
3 > 1 4 2 3 5 — 8 > 1 4 5 2 3

**8** (4) stayed (1) the tourist (3) yesterday (2) at a nice hotel
12 > 1 4 2 3 — 11 > 1 4 3 2

**9** (2) never (1) Mrs. Cod (3) eats (5) fish (4) on Friday
9 > 1 3 5 2 4 — 3 > 1 2 3 5 4

**10** (4) tonight (3) doing (2) you (1) what (5) are
20 > 3 2 4 1 5 — 9 > 1 5 2 3 4

**11** (4) you (3) gone (2) to the disco (1) ever (5) have

7 > 4 3 2 1 5 — 11 > 5 4 1 3 2

**12** (4) only (1) the mechanic (2) checked (3) the oil

13 > 1 2 4 3 — 7 > 1 4 2 3

**13** (1) the children (3) their toys (2) outside (4) left

18 > 1 4 3 2 — 16 > 1 3 2 4

**14** (1) know (2) I (3) here (4) the watch (5) is

16 > 2 1 3 4 5 — 14 > 2 1 4 5 3

**15** (3) everywhere (2) must (1) you (4) look

16 > 1 2 4 3 — 17 > 3 2 1 4

**16** (5) has (4) the money (3) my rich uncle (2) already (1) sent

17 > 3 5 2 1 4 — 15 > 3 5 1 2 4

**17** (4) arrived (1) the plane (2) early (3) quite

22 > 1 4 2 3 — 19 > 1 4 3 2

**18** (4) are (2) what (3) you (5) today (1) going to do

20 > 2 4 3 5 1 — 15 > 2 4 3 1 5

**19** (4) wait (2) for the concert (3) can (5) hardly (1) I

21 > 1 3 5 2 4 — 20 > 1 3 5 4 2

**20** (3) is (2) next (1) what (4) he (5) going to sing

23 > 1 3 4 5 2 — 24 > 1 2 3 4 5

**21** (4) he (5) given (3) his best concert (2) just (1) has

21 > 4 1 2 5 3 — 13 > 4 1 5 2 3

**22** (4) sometimes (1) the customs officer (2) your suitcase (3) opens

24 > 1 3 4 2 — 13 > 1 4 3 2

**23** (5) has (3) the smuggler (4) hidden (2) somewhere (1) the diamond

22 > 3 5 4 2 1 — 24 > 3 5 4 1 2

**24** (4) he (1) is (2) tomorrow (3) where (5) going to go

22 > 3 1 4 5 2 — 7 > 3 1 4 2 5

## Adverbs and Adjectives

***Wie muß es richtig heißen?***

1 That girl is — loud · 13 / louder · 16 — than ten elephants at a party.

2 She is as — noisily · 20 / noisy · 14 — as twenty monkeys in a cage.

3 I hope she is going to be — quiet · 5 / quietly · 22 — .

4 That was a very — hard · 3 / hardly · 23 — test.

5 My poor friend — nowhere · 11 / never · 12 — pays the bill.

6 The dance partners danced together — beautiful · 15 / beautifully · 1 — .

7 The woman danced especially — good · 19 / well · 8 — .

8 Harald was a — bad · 10 / badly · 24 — dancer because he had two left feet.

9 He — always · 18 / everywhere · 17 — stepped on his partner's foot.

10 The helicopter pilot flew — dangerous · 9 / dangerously · 23 — near the water.

11 The fire brigade has done a — fantastically · 2 / fantastic · 21 — job this year.

12 The exchange rate for the dollar dropped | quickly · 19 / quick · 6 | .

13 That man is a very | well · 5 / good · 4 | auto mechanic.

14 The thief | angrily · 2 / angry · 8 | left the house without anything.

15 We are | more worried · 6 / worriedly · 10 | than they are.

16 The | lazy · 15 / lazily · 21 | mechanic worked very slowly on my car.

17 Has he injured himself | bad · 14 / badly · 20 | ?

18 I love drinking | expensively · 3 / expensive · 17 | orange juice.

19 Look! That | crazy · 7 / crazily · 19 | man is climbing the skyscraper.

20 He has | almost · 22 / quite · 4 | climbed to the top of it.

21 Yes, you are | quite · 24 / never · 2 | right.

22 Now he is | excited · 17 / excitedly · 13 | jumping up and down.

23 The fire brigade is watching him | nervously · 9 / nervous · 5 | .

24 He | happy · 8 / happily · 11 | puts on a T-shirt with “The flying fat man” on it.

## The "Will"-Future

*Das* "Will-future" *bildet man mit* will + *Infinitiv. Beim* "Will-future" *handelt es sich entweder um einen Vorgang, der sich in der Zukunft ereignen wird* (It will rain soon.) *oder um einen spontanen Entschluß* (I'll help you.). *Im Deutschen ist dieses oft im Präsens ausgedrückt. Die Verneinung ist* "won't" / "will not".

**Put the following conversation in the correct tense: present / present perfect / past / future!**

1 Dad, the race starts at two o'clock. We ______ hurry.
will have to · 23 | had to · 7

2 Don't worry, son. ______ there before two o'clock.
We will be · 21 | We are · 17

3 Dad, ______ some petrol in the tank?
do you put · 19 | have you already put · 20

4 Yes, but I ______ to check the oil.
forget · 15 | forgot · 24

5 Don't worry, dad. Let me ______ it for you.
check · 14 | have checked · 22

6 ______ to come along, too?
Does your sister want · 22 | Has your sister wanted · 18

7 No, Maureen ______ any fun at the races this afternoon.
didn't have · 6 | won't have · 16

8 Why do you think she ______ them?
didn't like · 13 | won't like · 18

9 To tell the truth dad, she ______ motor-racing.
will hate · 8 | hates · 19

10 You are right son. Let's ______ her first.
will ask · 15 | ask · 13

11 Maureen, ______ downstairs for a moment, please?
can you come · 17 | did you come · 11

12 Just a moment, dad. I __________ down in a minute.
will be · 15 | am · 9

13 So here I am. What __________ you want?
will · 11 | do · 12

14 The motor-race __________ in about an hour.
has started · 8 | will start · 10

15 __________ to see the races?
Have you wanted · 3 | Do you want · 8

16 __________ you know dad? I hate motor-racing.
Don't · 11 | Won't · 9

17 Well Maureen, no one __________ home this afternoon.
was · 1 | will be · 3

18 Don't worry dad. Susan __________ over the afternoon.
can come · 7 | came · 4

19 I __________ her up and ask if she can come.
have rung · 5 | will ring · 4

20 Just a moment young girl! What __________ you two do here?
will · 5 | do · 1

21 Oh, we __________ our homework.
do · 9 | will do · 1

22 I __________ I can believe that.
won't think · 6 | don't think · 9

23 It's true. Our teacher __________ us to watch a film on TV!
will tell · 2 | told · 6

24 O.k. dear. Your brother and I __________ back at five o'clock.
will be · 2 | are · 24

## Clauses

*Ein Nebensatz* (clause) *kann durch folgende Konjunktionen eingeleitet werden:* because *(weil)*, so *(deshalb/damit)*, if *(wenn)*, when *(als)*, while *(während)*, unless *(wenn … nicht)*, before *(bevor)*.

***Bilde sinnvolle Nebensätze!***

1 ← The children can't go out,
- because it's raining. · 19
- so he dropped a glass. · 11

2 ← They sang,
- unless he does his homework. · 18
- while they were dancing. · 23

3 ← The picnic ended,
- when the sun went down. · 22
- if you can't cook. · 17

4 ← The bank clerk counted the money,
- while I waited. · 20
- before you go. · 13

5 ← Dad turned off the TV,
- because it was so late. · 15
- if you aren't good. · 24

6 ← Dad will turn on the TV,
- if you are good. · 24
- while I was here. · 17

7 ← I helped mum,
- while dad was working outside. · 18
- before Sheila gives him a book. · 16

8 ← We'll get in trouble,
- unless you are quiet. · 14
- when he was breaking the door. · 21

9 ← Let's play tennis,
- if the weather is nice. · 21
- while I'm washing the dishes. · 4

10 ← The computer stopped,
- so everyone went home. · 16
- unless the rain stops. · 2

11 ← Fat Freddy eats hamburgers,
- so they tasted good. · 9
- because they taste good. · 13

12 ← Marilyn kissed him,
- if he likes her. · 1
- before he went home. · 17

13 ← Mr. Pander will get off,
- when the bus stops. · 8
- while they ate lunch. · 12

14 ← Ben needed money,
- so he sold ice-cream. · 12
- because ice-cream tastes good. · 9

15 ← The monkey climbed the tree,
- so it could get a banana. · 9
- because it has lunch. · 7

16 ← The girl laughed,
- when Willy fell down. · 7
- so the traffic lights turned red. · 5

17 ← Caveman's dinosaur comes,
- when he calls it. · 5
- unless I was late. · 10

18 ← My aunt left,
- so we are late. · 6
- when my noisy cousins arrived. · 10

19 ← You won't forget it,
- if you write it down. · 6
- while they were eating. · 1

20 ← Willy broke his leg,
- if he was playing football. · 3
- while he was playing football. · 1

21 ← The shop will close,
- so they sell more things. · 11
- unless they sell more things. · 3

22 ← The rabbits ate carrots,
- unless the cows ate grass. · 2
- while the cows were eating grass. · 11

23 ← We drank cold tea,
- because it was so hot. · 2
- before it was so hot. · 4

24 ← There weren't any seats,
- so we had to stand. · 4
- because he plays tennis. · 15

## For / Since *(Für Fortgeschrittene)*

*Es gibt zwei englische Wörter für das deutsche Wort „seit“, und zwar* “for” *bei einem Zeitraum und* “since” *bei einem Zeitpunkt.*
*Wir benutzen das* Present Perfect *mit* for / since*:*
I have only watched TV for fifteen minutes.
He has been in Paris since Tuesday.

1 Kevin and Caveman have been outside ___ three hours.
for · 12 ___ since · 19 ___

2 Mum hasn’t seen them ___ breakfast.
since · 8 ___ for · 1 ___

3 Tanja has been in the disco ___ 8 o’clock this evening.
for · 9 ___ since · 10 ___

4 The poor dinosaur hasn’t eaten ___ five days.
since · 23 ___ for · 11 ___

5 They have known each other ___ a long time.
for · 3 ___ since · 23 ___

6 She has had her dog ___ Wednesday.
for · 14 ___ since · 7 ___

7 The dog has waited for her ___ two hours.
for · 1 ___ since · 13 ___

8 We have lived here ___ June.
for · 2 ___ since · 5 ___

9 The baby has been alone ___ two hours.
for · 9 ___ since · 24 ___

10 The geese haven’t been here ___ November.
since · 4 ___ for · 17 ___

11 My sister hasn’t had ice-cream ___ her birthday.
for · 21 ___ since · 6 ___

12 Professor Klinkenpot hasn't slept ______ two days.
since · 20 | for · 2

13 He has been in his time-machine ______ Monday.
since · 23 | for · 15

14 John and Nils haven't broken a window ______ May.
for · 11 | since · 19

15 The film star hasn't had to shake a hand ______ five hours.
since · 6 | for · 21

16 My parents have worried about it ______ Friday.
for · 12 | since · 24

17 She hasn't given a concert ______ her accident.
for · 16 | since · 14

18 He has thought about going there ______ two days.
since · 20 | for · 22

19 The baby-sitter has only left the room ______ one minute.
since · 4 | for · 13

20 The baby has worn wet clothes ______ dinner.
since · 18 | for · 8

21 The poor man hasn't paid his telephone bill ______ April.
for · 21 | since · 15

22 The women haven't talked to each other ______ six hours.
for · 20 | since · 13

23 I have kept the goldfish in my pocket ______ two days.
for · 17 | since · 5

24 Tim has had a toothache ______ 10 o'clock.
since · 16 | for · 12

## I'll be there on Time! (Prepositions)

**Put in the correct preposition!**

| | | | | |
|---|---|---|---|---|
| 1 | It's 6:45 a.m. and Kevin must get | up · 13 | on · 22 | . |
| 2 | Kevin wants to meet Caveman | in · 7 | at · 15 | 7:30. |
| 3 | His alarm clock is very loud, so he turns it | on · 21 | off · 6 | . |
| 4 | Then he goes | in · 3 | into · 2 | the bathroom. |
| 5 | Now he is standing | in front of · 11 | behind · 8 | the mirror. |
| 6 | He puts cold water | on · 4 | next to · 1 | his face and combs his hair. |
| 7 | His comb falls | out of · 9 | off · 16 | his hand onto the floor. |
| 8 | It is now lying | above · 5 | under · 7 | a chair. |
| 9 | Then he picks | off · 19 | up · 17 | the comb. |
| 10 | He takes | off · 24 | on · 10 | his pyjamas and dresses. |
| 11 | He must hurry, so he rushes | onto · 12 | into · 20 | the kitchen. |
| 12 | His mum has already put his breakfast | under · 14 | on · 22 | the table. |
| 13 | | In the middle · 1 | On the middle · 12 | of his plate there's some bacon and eggs. |
| 14 | | At · 19 | On · 3 | Saturday he usually has cornflakes with milk. |
| 15 | But today he must have something hot | before · 6 | for · 5 | breakfast. |
| 16 | During breakfast he hears his favourite song | at · 20 | on · 14 | the radio. |
| 17 | | After · 7 | Before · 21 | he leaves the kitchen he must wash his plate. |
| 18 | He puts his plate | on the top · 18 | at the top · 2 | of some other plates. |
| 19 | Then he looks | after · 24 | at · 10 | his watch and sees that he's late. |
| 20 | He opens the kitchen door and walks | after · 15 | through · 19 | it. |
| 21 | Now he has to look | at · 14 | for · 23 | his raincoat. |
| 22 | He finds it | behind · 16 | through · 23 | his bed. |
| 23 | The phone's ringing, so he picks | off · 17 | up · 8 | the telephone. |
| 24 | It's Caveman and he's ill | on · 9 | in · 12 | bed and can't come. |